0779056861

De
in

Michael Dean

Penguin Quick Guides Series Editors:
Andy Hopkins and Jocelyn Potter

PENGUIN ENGLISH

Pearson Education Limited
Edinburgh Gate
Harlow
Essex CM20 2JE, England
and Associated Companies throughout the world.

ISBN 0 582 46889 2

First published 2001
Text copyright © Michael Dean 2001

The moral right of the author has been asserted.

Produced for the publisher by Bluestone Press, Charlbury, UK.
Designed and typeset by White Horse Graphics, Charlbury, UK.
Illustrations by Sarah Wimperis (Graham-Cameron Illustration).
Photography by Patrick Ellis.
Printed and bound in Denmark by Norhaven A/S, Viborg.

All rights reserved; no part of this publication may be reproduced, stored in a retrieval system, or transmitted in any form or by any means, electronic, mechanical, photocopying, recording or otherwise, without the prior written permission of the Publishers.

Published by Pearson Education Limited in association with
Penguin Books Ltd, both companies being subsidiaries of Pearson plc.

To Mum and Dad with love and thanks.

For a complete list of the titles available from Penguin English visit our website at www.penguinenglish.com, or please write to your local Pearson Education office or to: Marketing Department, Penguin Longman Publishing, 5 Bentinck Street, London W1U 2EG.

Contents

Getting started   7

1 Describing objects   11
Shapes round • flat • square • rectangular • diamond-shaped
Positive really + *adj* • useful • extra + *adj* • high-quality
inexpensive • amazing
Negative go wrong • doesn't work • unsatisfactory • no good
keeps + -ing
Approximate kind of • sort of • about • *adj* + -ish
colour + y-*colour* • more or less
Comparing a bit like • -er than • too... • not ... enough • as ... as

2 Describing people   23
Size extremely + *adj* • average • pretty + *adj* • slim
overweight
Hair very + *adj* • dyed + *colour* • got a + *noun* • look + *adj* •
shaved head • completely + *adj*
Personality broad-minded • hard-working • big-headed
self-satisfied • not + *adj* + enough • strong-willed
Identifying in the middle • at the back • on the end
with long hair • in the hat
Reactions heartbroken • furious • fed up • pleased
thrilled to bits

3 Outside world   35
Weather pouring • blazing hot • freezing cold • a bit + *adj* chilly • windy
Towns and cities purpose-built • run-down • smashed boarded up • burnt-out • like + *noun phrase*
Mountains steep • wonderful • absolutely + *adj* breathtaking • rocky
Sea crescent-shaped • like + *noun* • calm • gentle • so + *adj* peaceful
Country neighbourly • more + *adj* • isolated • unreliable

4 House and home   47
Renting a flat self-contained • two-bedroom semi-detached • fully furnished • fitted
Living space airy • well-lit • spacious • open-plan • split-level
Room single • for (your computer) • with (two drawers) double • to (keep clothes in)
Kitchen gas • washing • electric • waste-disposal
Negative description cramped • hideous • terribly + *adj* messy • filthy

5 Emotions and states   59
Health fine • under the weather • poorly • seriously ill quite + *adj*
Emotions crazy about • in love with • confused about restless • depressed
Senses feel like • smell like • look like • sound like
Success extremely + *adv* • rapidly • successfully • remarkable

Failure disastrous • go + *adj* • out of order • more + *adv* in trouble

6 Movement and location 71
Direction straight ahead • from side to side • backwards forwards • diagonally
Walking walking • on foot • there and back • brisk I've got + *noun phrase*
Driving at a snail's pace • steady • at high speed like a lunatic • at a standstill
Location 1 in the foreground • in the corner in the background • in the distance • to the right
Location 2 central • miles from anywhere • in the middle of right opposite • convenient for

7 Performance 83
Jobs imaginative • enthusiastic • loyal • demanding well-paid
Work responsible for • involved in • answerable to impressed with
Leisure not bad at • fit • fantastic • dreadful • pretty + *adv*
Machines hi-tech • built-in • state-of-the-art • latest by remote control
Television wide-screen • digital • satellite • cable • interactive

8 Judgements 95
Food and drink delicious • tasty • bland • tasteless • spicy superb

Film and TV moving • beautifully shot • well acted • brilliant
tedious • incredibly + *adj*
Stories exciting • romantic • terrifying • too + *adj* + to
amusing
Possibility 1 100% certain • no doubt at all • confident
an outside chance • unlikely
Possibility 2 definitely • likely • probably • a chance of
possible

9 Time 107

Clock time coming up to • just after • around • precisely
Duration *number* + -hour • overnight • from … to
for a while • until
Sequence at the same time (as) • straight away • afterwards
previously • subsequently
Frequency on the hour • every + *length of time* • all the time
now and again • once a(n) + *time word*

10 Grammar reference 117

1 Adjectives: position   2 Adjectives: order   3 Adjectives plus
4 Adjectives: *-ing/-ed*   5 Adjectives: compounds
6 Adjectives: comparing 1   7 Adjectives: comparing 2
8 Verbs: *have got*   9 Verbs: + *like*   10 Verbs: purpose
11 Verbs: useful patterns   12 Adverbs   13 Prepositions
14 Approximate language

Index 135

Answers 158

Getting started

How can this book help you?

You can't get far in English before you need to describe something, whether it's the way you feel, the weather, or yesterday's TV programmes. But many learners of English use the same few general words and expressions again and again. *The Penguin Quick Guide to Descriptions in English* introduces you to a wide range of words, phrases and grammatical patterns that will help you to boost your word power and allow you to say what you really mean.

What's in this book?

This book has nine chapters that present descriptions in English in short, amusing texts and cartoons. Each chapter ends with a **Review** that tests your understanding. Answers to these exercises are in the **Answers** section. At the back of the book is an **Index** with example sentences using the descriptive words and phrases covered in the chapters. Descriptions in English often occur in particular grammar patterns and these patterns are explained in the **Grammar Reference** in chapter 10. The entries in the **Index** guide you to the relevant **Grammar Reference** page.

Why is this book called a *Quick Guide*?

Because it's short and guides you quickly to the words you need. For example, if you want to describe your most unusual birthday present, turn to *Describing objects*. Do you want to describe people? Turn to chapter 2, *Describing people*.

This is a *Quick Guide*. You don't need to spend hours studying it. Just look through it for ten minutes every day – and see how quickly you learn.

- Choose a chapter and read a text that interests you – you don't have to start at the beginning of the book.
- Look at the cartoon. It will help you to remember the text.
- If you want to learn how the grammar works, find the word in the **Index** and follow the number to the **Grammar Reference**.
- Next time just look at the texts. Next time just look at the pictures. Next time read the **Grammar Reference** or the **Index** first … it doesn't matter! Use your ten minutes a day with this book any way you like.

Have fun!

Describing objects

1

Shapes

round
flat
square
rectangular
diamond-shaped

Do you remember when music came on **round**, **flat** things made of plastic? They were called records and they were sold in **square** covers made of paper. Look at this old record player. No, don't laugh! Let's lift the **rectangular** plastic lid. This arm has a **diamond-shaped** needle in the end and when they put the needle on the record, music played. Yes, really! Can I ask you again to stop laughing!

This **flat**, **round** thing played music.

Positive

*An **amazing** twenty hours' playing time!*

HERE'S SOMETHING THAT'S **REALLY USEFUL!**

EXTRA-LONG VIDEO CASSETTES £10.95 for two!

Use them to video TV programmes when you go on holiday.

Extra-long video cassettes – ten hours long!

At £10.95 for two, these **high-quality** video cassettes are really **inexpensive** – an **amazing** twenty hours' playing time from a pack of two!

really + adj

useful

extra + adj

high-quality

inexpensive

amazing

Negative

*It **keeps** **printing** everything in Spanish.*

Hello? My computer's Internet access **goes wrong** all the time. When I go on the Internet I get my brother's e-mails. And the left speaker **doesn't work** – I can't hear anything on the left. Also the screen is **unsatisfactory** because it's too small. And the main tower is **no good** because it doesn't have a CD-ROM drive. And the printer … you never know what it's going to do! It was OK yesterday but now it **keeps printing** everything in Spanish.

go wrong

doesn't work

unsatisfactory

no good

keeps + -ing

Approximate

kind of

sort of

about

adj + -ish

colour+ y-colour

more or less

I left him on the London train. He's a **kind of** talking bear. You know, not a real talking bear, a soft toy! He's got a **sort of** … collar thing round his neck. He's **about** 20 centimetres long. You know, **smallish**. And a **yellowy-brown** colour. I'm alone in the world since my boyfriend left me and he's **more or less** the only friend I've got. I really love him.

He's **more or less** my only friend.

Comparing

VERONICA: I've just bought this silk shirt. It's **a bit like** your sister's, but it's **nicer than** hers.

TOM: You've already got a silk shirt, haven't you?

VERONICA: Yes, but I bought the other one five years ago! It's **too old-fashioned** now. And this one is for the evening. The other one isn't – it's **not smart enough**. I think I look **as pretty as** a picture in this!

TOM: Yes, darling. Of course you do!

---

a bit like

-er than

too …

not + adj + enough

as … as

Review 1

A Match 1–4 with a–e.

1 extra-large
2 square
3 high-quality
4 yellowy-brown

a) well-made
b) a shape
c) half-way between two colours
d) very big

B Put in the right form of cheap.

1 Cassettes are .... than CDs.
2 My clothes aren't as .... hers.
3 Sorry, that printer isn't .... enough for me.

C Are these good or bad about a computer?

1 It's unsatisfactory.
2 It keeps switching off.
3 It doesn't work at all.
4 It's faster than my last one.

Describing people

2

Size

extremely + adj

average

pretty + adj

slim

overweight

LONELY ♥ HEARTS
Meet new friends!

Your description of the man you are looking for:

I am looking for a man who is tall. Not **extremely tall**, just tall. I am a woman of **average** height but the only men I meet are **pretty short**. I'm looking down all the time. Also, please send me a **slim** man, NOT an **overweight** man, please!

*Yes, I'm **average** height. Are you free on Thursday?*

Hair

very + adj

dyed + colour

got a + noun

look + adj

shaved head

completely + adj

> Well, sir, your hair is black at the moment. **Very nice**. But a lot of footballers have **dyed blonde** hair, these days. Some have even **got a ponytail**. Or, if you want to **look tough**, you could have a **shaved head**. Look at David Beckham. He's playing brilliantly. You can't see any hair at all. He looks **completely** bald.

Personality

*I used to be **big-headed** but now I'm perfect.*

It was a good party. Tina was there. She laughed at all my jokes. She's very **broad-minded** – she doesn't get offended by anything. Danny arrived late, of course. He's really **hard-working**. And John was telling everybody how clever he is. That man is so **big-headed**. His wife is just as bad. She tells us how rich and happy and lucky she is all the time. She so **self-satisfied**! Oh and the diet's finished. I'm not strong-willed enough. After the party I helped Danny eat all the sandwiches that were left.

broad-minded

hard-working

big-headed

self-satisfied

strong-willed

Identifying

*Who's the man **in the hat**?*

30

Dear Alan

Sorry you couldn't be here in Nepal — hope you're feeling a bit better. Here's a photo of some of the people in our group. They're a strange lot! The woman **in the middle** is Jenny, an Australian, and the man behind her **at the back** is Pete, her husband. They're great fun. Then there's Ian — you remember him, don't you? He's the one in the shorts. That's his girlfriend Sasha next to him **on the end, with long hair**. And the man **in the hat**? I've no idea — he was just walking past when I took the picture!

in the middle

at the back

on the end

with long hair

in the hat

Reactions

heartbroken
furious
fed up
pleased
thrilled to bits

My little brother is **heartbroken** at the moment. His girlfriend just left him. I was **furious** with her, actually. She met another boy at a party and told Martin that after three years she was **fed up** with him and didn't want to see him any more. We were **pleased** to get your news, after all this time. Congratulations on the new job and Julia and I are **thrilled to bits** about your new baby. Fantastic news!

*Bob says he's **thrilled to bits** about the baby.*

Review 2

A Match 1–4 with a–d.
1 fed   a) working
2 big-   b) minded
3 hard-   c) headed
4 broad-   d) up

B Put in the missing word or phrase.
completely bald   overweight   average height
1 David is not tall and he's not short. He's .....
2 Mr Jackson has no hair at all. He's .....
3 I eat a lot so I'm .....

C True or false?
1 If you are furious, you are happy.
2 If you are thrilled to bits, you are very happy.
3 Dyed hair is always blonde.

Outside world

3

Weather

Holiday Diary

*November 15th – Venice: It's **pouring** with rain! Water everywhere. Can't go out.*

*November 16th – Athens: It's **blazing hot**! 38 degrees! Stayed in hotel room.*

*November 17th – Paris: It's **freezing cold**! Snow on the ground. Stayed in hotel room.*

*November 18th – Cannes: It's **a bit chilly**. Left my coat in Paris. Can't go out.*

*November 19th: Home at last! Very **windy**. A tree in the garden blew down.*

pouring

blazing hot

freezing cold

a bit + adj

chilly

windy

Towns and cities

I'm just going to the post office, OK?

BONHILL – WHAT WENT WRONG?

Thirty years ago, Bonhill was a modern, **purpose-built** suburban housing estate. It was a pleasure to live there. But in the last five years it has become one of the most **run-down** and dangerous parts of the city. Everywhere you go you see houses with **smashed** windows. And those that are not smashed are **boarded up** with wood. Here and there **burnt-out** cars lie **like leftovers from a war**. So what's gone wrong?

purpose-built

run-down

smashed

boarded up

burnt-out

like + noun phrase

Mountains

I don't think the view is **wonderful**.

Be quiet and eat your dinner.

THE SHANNON MOUNTAINS

At over 2,000 metres high, Mount Breen is the tallest of the Shannon mountain range. It is a **steep** climb to the top – at times the path seems almost vertical – but the view from the peak is **wonderful – absolutely breathtaking**. To the north is the **rocky** coastline; to the south you can look for miles across beautiful valleys.

steep

wonderful

absolutely + adj

breathtaking

rocky

Sea

... *you feel that nothing can go wrong ...*

> It's a lovely morning and I'm standing here on the beautiful **crescent-shaped** beach at Horton. The sea is **like glass** – **calm** and shining in the morning sun. There's a **gentle** breeze and there's not a cloud in the sky. It's **so peaceful**. On a morning like this you feel that nothing can go wrong …

crescent-shaped

like + noun

calm

gentle

so + adj

peaceful

Country

We regret to inform you that the 7.35 train to London will be delayed by three weeks.

*The trains are a bit **unreliable**.*

When I lived in London I had no idea who lived in the next house, but in this village people are very **neighbourly** – we're in and out of each other's houses all the time. And it's true that country people are **more friendly** – there seems to be more time to stop and talk. I couldn't live in an **isolated** house in the middle of a field, but living quietly in a small village suits me well. The only real problem is transport. There's a station in the village but the trains are a bit **unreliable**.

---

neighbourly

more + adj

isolated

unreliable

Review 3

A Match 1–4 with a–d.
1 boarded-up   a) cars
2 burnt-out   b) windows
3 breathtaking   c) breeze
4 gentle   d) view

B Match the sentences with phrases a–c.
1 It's pouring.   a) too warm
2 It's a bit chilly.   b) wet
3 It's blazing hot.   c) cold

C Which word is stronger?
1 a) nice   b) wonderful
2 a) breathtaking   b) beautiful
3 a) freezing   b) chilly

House and home

4

Renting a flat

So this is a quiet street!

FLATS TO RENT

AVAILABLE FROM OCTOBER 1st

Two **self-contained**, **two-bedroom** flats in a large **semi-detached** house in a quiet city centre street. Each flat is **fully furnished** with new furniture and **fitted** carpets throughout. £550 a month each.

Please call City Lets on 73102

---

self-contained

two-bedroom

semi-detached

fully furnished

fitted

Living space

airy
well-lit
spacious
open-plan
split-level

1 Acacia Avenue

MAIN ROOM

The main room is **airy** and **well-lit** with three large windows overlooking the street. It is extremely **spacious** – eight metres by five – and contains **open-plan** dining and seating areas. Two steps from the dining area take you down into the seating area. A beautiful **split-level** living space!

*The Robinsons were told the house was **split level** ...*

Room

single

for (your computer)

with (two drawers)

double

to (keep clothes in)

Student Handbook

ACCOMMODATION

Each student room in the college has the same furniture:

- a **single** bed
- a desk **for your computer**
- a cupboard **with two drawers** and three shelves
- a **double** wardrobe **to keep clothes in**

Most students soon make their room feel like home.

Kitchen

I think you should have removed the knives and forks first …

Student Handbook

KITCHEN FACILITIES

Students share a kitchen. Each kitchen includes:
- a fridge – please do not unplug it!
- a **gas** cooker – please clean it after use!
- a **washing** machine – put £1 in when you want to wash your clothes.
- an iron and ironing board – please put these away after use.
- a large **electric** kettle – makes six cups.
- a **waste-disposal** unit in the sink – please use this ONLY for left-over food.

gas

washing

electric

waste-disposal

Negative description

cramped

hideous

terribly + adj

messy

filthy

Dear Mum

Here I am in my new room. It's really **cramped** – tiny. And the walls are a **hideous** colour – sort of yellowy-green. The kitchen – which I share with five other students – is **terribly messy** and the bathroom's **filthy**. I think I'm going to like it here!

Sorry, it's a bit **cramped** in here.

Review 4

A Match 1–4 with a–d.
1 self-　　a) messy
2 terribly　b) level
3 open-　　c) contained
4 split-　　d) plan

B Put in the missing words.
washing machine   filthy   open-plan   split-level
1 Their house is .... – the front is much lower than the back.
2 This T-shirt's ..... Put it in the .....
3 Let's knock down the wall between the kitchen and the sitting room and make it .....

C Add for, with or to
1 There's a cupboard .... keep your food in.
2 There's a wardrobe .... your clothes.
3 There's a cooker .... four gas rings on it.

Emotions and states

5

Health

Henry? No, unfortunately Henry is **fine**.

JESSICA: How are the children?

SARAH: Henry is **fine**, no problems there. But William is a bit **under the weather** – nothing serious but he's got a cold.

JESSICA: Oh dear. And Lauren?

SARAH: Lauren, I'm afraid, is really **poorly**. She's been ill for days. Claire's not very well either. She's feeling very weak and she can't eat anything. But she'll be OK by the end of the week – she's not **seriously ill**. What's your news?

JESSICA: Nothing interesting … We're all **quite healthy** … .

---

fine

under the weather

poorly

seriously ill

quite + adj

Emotions

Tea, Emma?

Tea? Tea? I'm **in love** and all you can talk about is tea!

I don't know what to do about Tony. His girlfriend's **crazy about** him, but he isn't really **in love with** her. He's very **confused about** the whole situation. One day he loves her, the next day he doesn't. So he's very **restless** and he's doing badly at school. He's getting bad marks and that makes him **depressed**. He won't talk to me. Could you try?

crazy about

in love with

confused about

restless

depressed

63

Senses

feel like
smell like
look like
sound like

MY SPECIAL FRIEND

Her hair **feels like** silk – soft and smooth.

She **smells like** autumn, dark and strong.

She **looks like** a lioness – so proud and alone.

But she **sounds like** a baby when she cries.

I am her world and she is mine.

... I am her world and she is mine.
Poetry
The world of the senses
Is this about your girlfriend?
No – my new dog!

Success

"Here's your pocket money, dad."

*Eric's computer business is doing **extremely well**.*

ABELMAN DESIGN IN THE USA

– by a Daily News reporter

Abelman Design is doing **extremely well** in America. Jenny Abelman started her own clothes company in New York two years ago and since then, the company has grown **rapidly**. It has **successfully** changed from a very small company to one that employs more than 500 people. 'The last two years have been **remarkable** and the future looks bright for us,' said Jenny as she introduced her new fashion collection in the Henley Building.

extremely + adv

rapidly

successfully

remarkable

Failure

Don't worry. We'll be in New York in four hours.

Dear Roger,

I'm writing to you about Paul. He opened a small sandwich and cake shop last year but it was **disastrous** right from the start. In the first week, his coffee machine **went wrong** – it was **out of order** for weeks. But the real problems started when the supermarket next door began selling sandwiches and cakes **more cheaply** than Paul's. He was really **in trouble** from then on. He had to close the shop last week and he's lost everything. Is there anything we can do? He is our nephew, after all.

disastrous

go + adj

out of order

more + adv

in trouble

Review 5

A Match 1–4 with a–d.
1 in love
2 confused
3 under
4 out of

a) order
b) the weather
c) about
d) with

B Are you happy or unhappy?
1 I'm in a disastrous marriage.
2 I'm feeling restless.
3 I'm crazy about my job.

C Are these true or false?
1 People who are under the weather are not feeling well.
2 If your business goes wrong you are in trouble.
3 If you're seriously ill, you'll soon be better.

Movement and location

6

Direction

Did you hear something then?

EYE-WITNESS REPORT

Everything seemed fine. The traffic was moving freely and I drove **straight ahead** on to the bridge. I was about half-way across when suddenly there was a huge noise – like a bomb going off – and the bridge began to move **from side to side**. My car started rolling **backwards** as the movement of the bridge became more violent. Then, quite suddenly, we were thrown **forwards** and our car went **diagonally** into the car in front. It was terrifying, but fortunately we weren't injured.

straight ahead

from side to side

backwards

forwards

diagonally

Walking

walking	Slimmer of the month Sid Brady is a **walking** miracle. He's lost five kilos in four weeks. How did he do it? 'I sold my car and I go everywhere **on foot** now,' said slim Sid. 'Before, I used to take the car everywhere – even to the corner shop. But now I walk **there and back**.' And does he enjoy it? 'Oh, yes. I go for a **brisk** walk every day – it's great. But **I've** been walking so much that **I've got** holes in my shoes!'
on foot	
there and back	
brisk	
has/ have got	

I'm just popping out to the shop.

Driving

MOTORWAYS – A GUIDE TO TYPES OF DRIVER

- THE SNAIL   Drives **at a snail's pace** in the inside lane – never faster than 50 kilometres per hour.

- THE 'GOOD' DRIVER   Drives at a **steady** 100kph. Never leaves the middle lane – causing lots of problems to other drivers.

- THE IDIOT   Drives **at high speed** at all times.

- THE MADMAN   Ignores the rules of the road and drives **like a lunatic**.

- THE DRIVER FROM ANOTHER PLANET   The traffic is **at a standstill** so he and his family get out and have a picnic in the emergency lane!

---

at a snail's pace

steady

at high speed

like + noun phrase

at a standstill

Location 1

In the foreground we can see a woman in a chair. The room is dark and empty – perhaps this represents the artist's memory of his unhappy childhood. **In the** top left-hand **corner** is a clock with no hands – this is a timeless picture. **In the background** is an open window, and outside it's raining. As we look through the window, we can see a lonely boy **in the distance**. Perhaps this is the artist himself. **To the right** of the boy is a phone box. What does it all mean? Well …

in the foreground
in the corner
in the background
in the distance
to the right

Location 2

central

miles from anywhere

in the middle of

right opposite

convenient for

They said our new office building was **central** – near the centre of town, near the train station. It's actually **miles from anywhere**. There's nothing here. It's **in the middle of** a field! There's one small house **right opposite** our building but otherwise … nothing. They also said it was **convenient for** shops and restaurants. There are no shops and restaurants anywhere near it!

It's **convenient for** the airport, anyway.

Review 6

A Do these phrases mean fast or slow?
1 at a snail's pace
2 like a lunatic
3 brisk

B Match 1–3 with a–c.
1 There's a town in the distance.
2 There's a shop right opposite my house.
3 The hotel is miles from anywhere.
a) There are no buildings near it.
b) It's very near.
c) It's quite far away.

C Complete these sentences.
on foot   convenient for   in the distance
1 I'll go ..... I need the exercise.
2 Look! There's the castle. You can see it ..... .
3 I live in the centre. It's .... shopping.

Performance

7

Jobs

*She seems quite **enthusiastic**.*

Infomania needs a SALES EXECUTIVE for its Data Services Division

We are looking for an IT-qualified person who is …

- **imaginative** – you must be able to bring your own ideas to the job
- **enthusiastic** – we want you to be excited about developing the business
- **loyal** – we want you to become an important part of our team on a long-term basis

This is a **demanding** job, involving hard work and long hours. In return, you will be **well-paid** (starting salary £35,000 pa) and will have immense job satisfaction.

Contact jeff@infomania

---

imaginative

enthusiastic

loyal

demanding

well-paid

Work

> You can have the cheese and the ham if I can have the chicken.

She is often **involved in** important negotiations.

John is Personal Assistant to the boss at Infomania. He is **responsible for** arranging her schedule and her travel. She's often **involved in** important negotiations and he has to make sure she has all the information she needs. Although she's the boss, she's **answerable to** the shareholders, because Infomania is a public company. John has only had the job for six months, but his boss must be **impressed with** his work because he's just had a salary increase.

responsible for

involved in

answerable to

impressed with

Leisure

not bad at

fit

fantastic

dreadful

pretty + adv

Dick's got a lot of hobbies. He's **not bad at** chess. He's also very **fit**. He goes jogging every morning and goes to the gym three times a week. He plays tennis too. He's got a **fantastic** serve. It comes over the net at about 100kph. I'm a **dreadful** player and I always lose to him. Then there's cooking. He cooks **pretty well**. He usually makes Italian food at dinner parties.

OK, Dick. You can serve now.

*Dick's got a **fantastic** serve.*

Machines

hi-tech

built-in

state-of-the-art

latest

by remote control

Chloe loves machines. She's got a **hi-tech** car with a talking computer. Her camera has a **built-in** infra-red flash that allows you to take pictures at night. She has a **state-of-the-art** WAP phone that connects to the Internet and, of course, she's got all the **latest** computer equipment. She's just bought a watch that lets her operate everything in her house **by remote control**. She doesn't even have to be in the house!

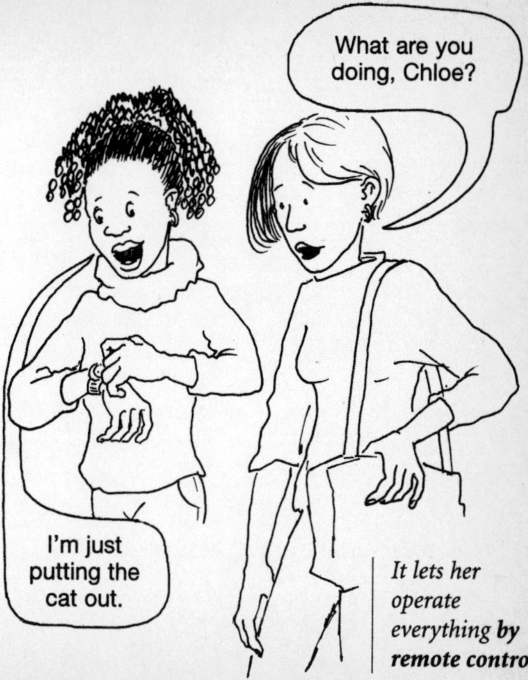

It lets her operate everything ***by remote control.***

Television

*It's even worse when the team loses on a **wide-screen** TV!*

MAN: This is a **wide-screen** TV. It's four metres by two.

CHLOE: Has it got **digital** sound?

MAN: Oh, yes – the sound and the pictures are much better than the old system.

CHLOE: Does it get **satellite** TV and **cable**?

MAN: We can put up a satellite dish for you. Or you can get cable TV if you live in the right area.

CHLOE: What about **interactive** television? I want to choose the endings of the programmes I watch.

MAN: Er ... It doesn't really work like that ...

wide-screen

digital

satellite

cable

interactive

Review 7

A Match 1–4 with a–d.
1 hi-   a) paid
2 well-   b) in
3 built-   c) screen
4 wide-   d) tech

B Put in the missing words.
in   to   by
1 I'm self-employed, so I'm not answerable .... anyone.
2 She can close her curtains .... remote control.
3 She's getting involved .... local politics.

C True or false?
1 The latest idea is a new idea.
2 If someone's impressed with your work, they hate it.
3 A dreadful cook is a good one.

Judgements

8

Food and drink

*Fiona likes **spicy** food and she is glad that Gavin does, too.*

GAVIN: That meal was absolutely **delicious**, Fiona, thank you. It was the best meal I've had for months. I thought the chicken was really **tasty**. Sometimes chicken tastes a bit **bland**, but yours was excellent.

FIONA: Thank you, Gavin. I'm so pleased. I know chicken can be a bit **tasteless** sometimes. But we all like **spicy** food and I'm glad you do, too. My spicy chicken wasn't too hot for you?

GAVIN: Oh no! And that was a **superb** wine, too.

delicious
tasty
bland
tasteless
spicy
superb

Film and TV

Cold Fish *was a slow and **tedious** film.*

FILM REVIEW

THE RED HAND
Director Arthur Ricks (205 minutes)

I thought *The Red Hand* was a really **moving** film. I was so moved that I cried! It was also **beautifully shot**. Some of the scenes of London in the early morning were as beautiful as anything I have ever seen in a cinema. It was also very **well acted**. Graham Peters and Stella Gerrard were **brilliant** as the main characters. All this was a nice surprise because the same director, Arthur Ricks, made that **tedious** film, *Cold Fish*, last year and I thought that was **incredibly slow**, with little action and even less emotion.

moving

beautifully shot

well acted

brilliant

tedious

incredibly + adj

Stories

These horror stories are great – but nothing like that happens in real life!

ROBERT: Personally, I like adventure stories – stories with a lot of action set in exotic places. A good story – whether it's a book or a film – has to be **exciting**.

RACHEL: I prefer **romantic** stories – you know, boy meets girl.

ROBERT: Not me. I enjoy horror stories, too. When I was young I found horror stories **terrifying** – I remember I was **too frightened to** go to bed after reading Dracula. But now I like them because they're **amusing** – well, they make me laugh anyway!

exciting

romantic

terrifying

too + adj + to

amusing

Possibility 1

Mr Jones has **no doubt at all** that today is going to be a good day.

MEMO from the Managing Director to all staff

We all know that the firm has had problems over the last year but we are **100% certain** that these problems have been overcome. There is **no doubt at all** that there are better times ahead for the firm. Our local business is already doing well, and we are **confident** that export sales will begin to improve before the end of the year. There's **an outside chance** that there will be a problem with one of our new products – but our marketing team is confident that that is very **unlikely**.

100% certain

no doubt at all

confident

an outside chance

unlikely

Possibility 2

definitely
likely
probably
a chance of
possible

THIS WEEK'S WEATHER

We've had quite a good week, but cooler, wetter weather is on its way. It will **definitely** be cold throughout the country tomorrow and snow is **likely** in the north. On Tuesday there will **probably** be rain in most of the south-east and there's **a chance of** storms and strong winds across the whole of the south on Wednesday and Thursday. More snow is **possible** at the weekend.

I don't care if there is **a chance** of snow. We're on holiday!

Review 8

A Put these in order of least to most certain.
1 likely
2 possible
3 100% certain
4 unlikely

B Are these good or bad?
1 a moving film
2 a superb wine
3 a tasteless meal

C Do you agree or disagree?
1 In romantic stories, people fall in love.
2 Spicy food can sometimes be a bit bland.
3 If something is 100% certain there is an outside chance that it will happen.
4 Most people like slow and tedious films.

Time

9

Clock time

coming up to

just after

around

precisely

Right! It's **coming up to** two o'clock, so I want you all to get on the bus. We're a little late so we'll leave **just after** two. We should get to Windsor Castle at **around** three, depending on the traffic. We only have two hours there, so please be back on the bus at five o'clock **precisely** for the journey back to Oxford.

They arranged to meet at 11 o'clock *precisely*.

Duration

number + -hour

overnight

from ... to

for a while

until

Fax

This is just to let you know that after a **six-hour** flight, I arrived safely. I'm staying **overnight** in Delhi because my meeting is **from** nine **to** twelve tomorrow morning. Then I'm free **for a while** before my flight to Bombay. I'll be at the Metropole Hotel in Bombay **until** Friday if you need to contact me.

Darling! Jack and Carol and the kids are staying **overnight**.

Sequence

*The teacher spoke and we took notes **at the same time**.*

Saint Simon's School Magazine

When I was at school things were very different from today. Learning had to be hard work. We had to suffer! There was no attempt to make lessons interesting. The teacher spoke and we took notes **at the same time**. If he or she asked you a question, you had to answer **straight away**. If you did anything wrong you had to stay at school **afterwards** for an extra hour. Fortunately, teachers weren't allowed to hit pupils. **Previously**, it had been a normal part of school life. I didn't enjoy school at all but I went to university and **subsequently** became a teacher! Now I'm back in school!

at the same time (as)

straight away

afterwards

previously

subsequently

Frequency

Two minutes to go!

*The baby needs a nappy change **every five minutes**.*

At the moment Jessie has to feed the new baby every hour, **on the hour** – so she can't really go out. And he seems to need a nappy change **every five minutes** – that's what it feels like anyway. The first week he seemed to cry **all the time**, but **now and again** he does sleep for a few hours at night. We're planning to get a baby-sitter and go out about **once a month**. If we don't we'll go crazy!

on the hour

every + length of time

all the time

now and again

once a + time word

Review 9

A Match 1–4 with a–d.
1 at the same time   a) again
2 straight   b) month
3 now and   c) as
4 once a   d) away

B Put in the missing words.
at the same time as   to   straight away   overnight
1 We were at home from 7.30 .... 10 o'clock.
2 We had to do what the teacher said .....
3 At school, we couldn't talk .... the teacher.
4 We stayed .... at our friends' house.

C True or false?
1 It's coming up to four o' clock now. (It's 4.05.)
2 It's just after four o'clock now. (It's 4.05.)
3 It's precisely four o'clock now. (It's 4.05.)

Grammar reference

10

1 Adjectives: position

Adjective + noun

This is probably the most common way of describing in English. Adjectives usually go **before** nouns in English and are often preceded by intensifiers. They often occur in patterns like this.

Determiner	Intensifier	Adjective(s)	Noun
a(n)	very	young	man
the	extremely	beautiful	painting
some	really	expensive	cars
a lot of	quite	cheap	books

Verb + adjective

Adjectives often occur after these verbs: *be, appear, prove, seem, small, become, get, go, grow, keep, remain, stay, turn*. They also occur after **sense** verbs: *feel, taste, look, sound*.

Verb	Intensifier	Adjective
It's		round
It's	(incredibly)	loud
It's getting	(pretty)	expensive
They're becoming	(extremely)	old
I feel	(very)	pleased
He's gone		crazy about her

2 Adjectives: order

Adjectives often occur in the following order:

1 Adjectives that describe a **quality** of someone or something: e.g. *tall, rich, hot, dirty*. People or things can have more or less of the quality.

2 Colour adjectives: *blue, green, yellowish, bluey-grey*.

3 **Classifying** adjectives ... that tell you about the class that something belongs to: *American, urban, foreign, modern*.

Here are some examples:

	Quality	**Colour**	**Classifying**	
A very	beautiful	blue	Chinese	plate
The	warm	blue	Mediterranean	sea

3 Adjectives plus

Adjective + preposition

A number of adjectives are followed by particular prepositions.

Here is a list of some common patterns:

answerable to	excited about/by	involved in
bored with	frightened of/by	kind to
careful with	happy with	polite to
crazy about	impressed with/by	protective of
cruel to	interested in	responsible to/for
depressed about/by		surprised by
		tired of

4 Adjectives: *ing/-ed*

-ing/-ed adjectives

Adjectives ending in *–ing* often describe **actions**.

A talking clock
A singing bird

A winning team
A laughing child

Adjectives ending in *–ed* (or a past participle form) often describe **states**.

A smashed window.
A painted box.

A lost child.
A surprised look.

5 Adjectives: compounds

Compound adjectives

A compound adjective is made of at least two words. Here are some words that you can put before some adjectives to make compound adjectives: *extra, semi, half, fully, well, badly*. Look at these examples.

extra-long   semi-detached   half-finished
fully furnished   well/badly dressed

Here are some other common compound adjectives:

bad-tempered   four-door   heart-shaped
world-famous   American-born   dark-haired
high-priced   English-speaking

6 Adjectives: comparing 1

Comparing 1

The basic rule is:

	comparative	superlative
one-syllable adjectives (small)	+ er (smaller)	+ est (smallest)
longer adjectives (sensitive)	+ more (more sensitive)	+ the most (the most sensitive)
adverbs (quietly)	+ more (more quietly)	+ the most (the most quietly)

Exceptions:

1 Some two-syllable adjectives always form comparative and superlative with *-er/-est*: *clever (clever/the cleverest) happy (happier/the happiest) quiet (quieter/quietest)*

   The opposite of some two-syllable words (like *happy*) can form the comparative and superlative in the same way: *unhappy (unhappier/the unhappiest)*

2 Some two-syllable adjectives can form the comparative and superlative with *-er/-est* OR *more/the most*:

polite	*politer*	*the politest*
OR	*more polite*	*most polite*
common	*commoner*	*the commonest*
OR	*more common*	*most common*

3 The most common irregular comparative forms are:

   good   better   the best   bad   worse   the worst

7 Adjectives: comparing 2

Comparing 2

Some of the most common ways of describing by comparing involve using similes, and using *not* + adj + *enough* and *too* + adj + *to*

comparing	It was a heart-shaped card.
Examples:	heart-shaped, U-shaped, egg-shaped
similes (as … as)	The house was as pretty as a picture.
Examples:	quiet/mouse, white/sheet, strong/ox, blind/bat, dry/bone
not + adj + enough	The desk wasn't big enough for the computer.
too + adj (+ to)	The computer was too big (to go on the desk).

8 Verbs: *have got*

Has/have got

This is another very common way of describing in English. *Have got* is often followed by:

a noun	He's got a ponytail.
a noun phrase	It's got a diamond-shaped needle. He's got blond hair.
a noun and a prepositional phrase	She's got a ring in her nose.
a noun and a relative clause	It's got a speaker that doesn't work.

9 Verbs: + *like*

We often use *like* in description. *Like* is followed by a noun phrase.

She sings like an angel.
They're good friends. They're like brothers.

We also use sense verbs + *like*.

look like	He looks like an old man, but he's only 30.
sound like	There's so much noise from the party upstairs. They sound like a herd of elephants.
smell like	This milk smells like cheese. How old is it?
taste like	I don't know what meat this is. It tastes like chicken.
feel like	This feels like silk. But actually, it's cotton.

10 Verbs: purpose

We often want to describe something by saying what its purpose is. One way of doing this is to use *to* + verb infinitive.

There is a wardrobe to keep your clothes in.

It has a button on the front to turn the machine on and off.

The new model has an airbag to protect you and your family.

You can also use the preposition *for* to describe purpose (see **13 Prepositions**).

11 Verbs: useful patterns

Patterns with verbs like *go*, *work* and *keep* are often used in description. *Go wrong* is often used with a frequency adverb like *often* or *all the time*. *Keeps + -ing* is usually used to describe something negative.

go + adj	e.g. **go wrong** It often goes wrong. It goes wrong all the time. e.g. **go bald** He's going bald.
doesn't work	It doesn't work at all. It works badly.
keeps + -ing	The car keeps breaking down. He keeps doing the wrong homework.

12 Adverbs

Adverbs say something more about a verb. They are often formed by adding *-ly* to an adjective (beautiful – *beautifully*). The main types of adverb are:

Manner These describe **how** something is done/happens. He played terribly.

Place These describe **where** something is done/happens.
The bridge went from side to side.

Time These describe **when** something is done/happens. Let's meet tomorrow at six.

Frequency These describe **how often** something is done/happens. I never go on planes.

Most intensifiers (*very, pretty, quite, incredibly,* etc.) can come before adverbs as well as adjectives (see **Grammar Reference 1 and 2**).

13 Prepositions

Prepositions often introduce a phrase that helps to identify something – perhaps by describing a characteristic, by saying where something is or what it is for. Here are some examples.

Characteristic The woman with long hair.
　　　　　　　　　The man in the hat.

Location The house in the middle.
　　　　　　The boy at the back.
　　　　　　The building on the end.

Purpose A shelf for your computer.
　　　　　　A wardrobe for keeping your clothes in.

14 Approximate language

People use approximate language very often when they speak, and it will make your English sound realistic.

kind of/ sort of
Use these before adjectives or nouns.
It's a sort of talking clock.

colour +y-colour
Use this to combine two colours.
The sky was a beautiful bluey-pink colour.

a bit
Use this to mean *a little*.
£100 was a bit more than I wanted to pay.

stuff   Use this in place of any uncountable noun.
Put that stuff on the floor, would you? I'll look at it later.

-ish   Use this on the end of most adjectives, particularly for colour and size.
He was tallish but not all that tall.
The walls are painted in a yellowish colour.

Index

Index

Each entry in the Index is followed by one or more numbers. These numbers refer to particular pages in the Grammar Reference in chapter 10. Turn to the relevant page and learn more about how the word or phrase is used. One or two phrases have no number.

Your language

100% certain 1
It's 100% certain that I'll come.
_____

a bit + adj 14
It's a bit cold, isn't it?
_____

a bit like 9/14
He looks a bit like his mother.
_____

about 13/14
She's about twenty-five, I think.
_____

absolutely + adj 1
The film was absolutely wonderful.
_____

a chance of
There's a chance of rain.
_____

afterwards 12
We ate and watched TV afterwards.
_____

Index

Your language

airy 1
It's an airy room. _____

all the time 12
She's two but she speaks all the time. _____

amazing 1
It's amazing! Her CD sold a million. _____

amusing 1
It's an amusing book. I laughed a lot. _____

an outside chance 1
There's an outside chance of snow. _____

answerable to 3
His boss is Pat. He's answerable to her. _____

around 13/14
I'll be there around three. _____

as ... as 7
I am as good as you at tennis. _____

at a snail's pace 12/13
He drives at a snail's pace – very slowly. _____

at a standstill
The traffic was at a standstill. _____

Index

Your language

at high speed 12/13
The car raced away at high speed.

at the back 12/13
We were at the back and couldn't see.

at the same time as 12/13
I finished at the same time as Dick.

average 1
He's not short; he's average height.

backwards 12
The car rolled backwards.

beautifully shot 5
The film was beautifully shot.

big-headed 5
Simon is really big-headed.

bland 1
It was so bland; it tasted of nothing.

blazing hot 1
It was blazing hot – 30 degrees.

boarded up 4/5
The windows are all boarded up.

Index

Your language

breathtaking 1
The view from Everest is breathtaking. _____

brilliant 1
Memoirs of a Geisha is a brilliant book. _____

brisk 1
He went for a brisk walk. _____

broad-minded 5
I'm broad-minded; you can't shock me. _____

built-in 4/5
The stereo system has built-in speakers. _____

burnt-out 4/5
There's a burnt-out car on the corner. _____

by remote control 12/13
The doors open by remote control. _____

cable 1
Have you got cable TV in your area? _____

calm 1
The sea was completely calm. _____

central 1
The hotel is central. _____

Index

Your language

chilly 1
Put a jacket on. It's chilly. _____

colour + y + colour 14
His shirt is bluey-green. _____

coming up to 14
It's just coming up to four o'clock. _____

completely + adj 1
He's got no hair – he's completely bald. _____

confident 1
We are confident that you will do well. _____

confused about 3
She's confused about Jake. _____

convenient for 3
The cottage is convenient for the shops. _____

cramped 1
The room is very cramped – it's tiny. _____

crazy about 3
I'm crazy about 60s music – I love it! _____

crescent-shaped 4/5
The moon is often crescent-shaped. _____

Index

	Your language
definitely 12	
I am definitely going to the party.	_____
delicious 1	
Judith cooks delicious food.	_____
demanding 4	
It's a demanding job.	_____
depressed 1	
He got depressed when his dog died.	_____
diagonally 12	
We walked diagonally across the field.	_____
diamond-shaped 4/5	
It's a diamond-shaped picture.	_____
digital 1	
All new TVs will be digital.	_____
disastrous 1	
6–0! What a disastrous game!	_____
doesn't work 11	
My watch doesn't work. It's broken.	_____
double 1	
They have a double wardrobe each.	_____

Index

Your language

dreadful 1
I've had a dreadful day. _____

dyed + colour 4/5
She's got dyed blonde hair. _____

electric 1
Do you prefer electric cookers to gas? _____

enthusiastic 1
I'm very enthusiastic about my job. _____

-er than 6
A palmtop is smaller than a laptop. _____

every + length of time 12
There's a bus every twenty minutes. _____

exciting 1
It was a really exciting film. _____

extra + adj 5
The extra-long tapes play for ten hours. _____

extremely + adj 1
He's extremely tall – over two metres! _____

extremely + adv 12
She plays extremely badly. _____

Index

Your language

fantastic 1
She's a fantastic tennis player.

fed up 1
I'm not happy at all, I'm fed up.

feel like 9
This present feels like a pullover.

filthy 1
His room isn't just dirty – it's filthy.

fine 1
Jane was ill but she's fine now.

fit 1
He runs to keep fit.

fitted 4
The flat has fitted carpets.

flat 1
I like flat land; you can see for miles.

for 13
This socket is for my computer.

for a while 12/13
You go. I'll stay here for a while.

Index

Your language

forwards 12
The car rolled forwards.
_____

freezing cold 4/5
It's freezing cold. Wear a scarf.
_____

from side to side 12
The bridge swung from side to side.
_____

from ... to 13
Breakfast is from seven to eight thirty.
_____

fully furnished 4/5
The flat's fully furnished.
_____

furious 1
John was furious.
_____

gas 1
I don't want a gas cooker.
_____

gentle 1
There was a warm and gentle breeze.
_____

go + adj 11
He went crazy.
_____

go wrong (machines) 11
My computer's always going wrong.
_____

Index

Your language

hard-working 4/5
Tina's very hard-working.
_____

has/have got 8
It's got a diamond-shaped needle.
_____

heartbroken 4/5
Fred's heartbroken because his dog died.
_____

hideous 1
The wallpaper is a hideous colour.
_____

high-quality 5
This TV has a high-quality picture.
_____

hi-tech 5
WAP phones are very hi-tech devices.
_____

imaginative 1
We need imaginative people.
_____

impressed with 3
Her boss was impressed with her work.
_____

incredibly + adj 1
It's incredibly hot in Spain in August.
_____

inexpensive 1
The wine was inexpensive. It cost £3.
_____

Index

Your language

in love with 13
Tim is in love with Sue. _____

interactive 1
It's an interactive game show. _____

in the background 12/13
There's a house in the background. _____

in the corner 12/13
There's a desk in the corner of the room. _____

in the distance 12/13
We could see a ship in the distance. _____

in the foreground 12/13
I'm in the foreground of the picture. _____

in the hat 13
The man in the hat is my brother. _____

in the middle (of) 12/13
I'm in the middle (of the picture). _____

in trouble 13
Some Internet businesses are in trouble. _____

involved in 3
She's involved in the football club. _____

Index

	Your language

-ish 14
He's not very tall, just tallish.

isolated 1
The house is isolated and lonely.

just after 12/13
It's just after three o'clock.

keeps + -ing 11
My CD player keeps stopping.

kind of 14
It's a kind of shop – well, a market stall.

latest 6
He always buys the latest car.

like + noun phrase 9
He cried like a baby.

likely 1
It's likely to snow in the mountains.

look + adj 1
Darren looks ill.

look like 9
It looks like a diamond but it's glass.

Index

Your language

loyal 1
Jack is a loyal employee. _____

messy 1
I hate living with messy people. _____

miles from anywhere 12
Their house is miles from anywhere. _____

more + adj 6
Country people are more friendly. _____

more + adv
He plays more beautifully than her. _____

more or less 14
He's more or less my only friend. _____

moving 4
It's a very moving film. It made me cry. _____

neighbourly 1
The Smiths are very neighbourly. _____

next door 5/12
He lives next door to us. _____

no doubt at all
I have no doubt at all that we will win. _____

Index

Your language

no good 1
This printer is no good. It's broken.

not + adj + enough 7
This jacket is not smart enough.

not bad at 1
He's not bad at tennis.

now and again 12
We eat out now and again.

number + hour 5
It's a three-hour journey.

once a + time word 12
I play tennis once a week, on Mondays.

on foot 12/13
There were no buses so we went on foot.

on the end 12/13
The boy on the end is my son.

on the hour 12/13
Trains leave on the hour, every hour.

open-plan 5
I work in an open-plan office.

Index

Your language

out of order 13
I'm sorry, the machine's out of order. _____

overnight 12
Why don't you stay overnight? _____

overweight 1
Don't eat so much – you're overweight. _____

peaceful 1
It's very peaceful in our little village. _____

pleased 1
I was really pleased to see Jean again. _____

poorly 1
David is poorly. He's in bed. _____

possible 1
It's possible that he'll come. _____

pouring 4
Don't go out in the pouring rain. _____

precisely 1
The time is precisely 7.18. _____

pretty + adj 1
He's a pretty good player. _____

Index

Your language

pretty + adv 12
John cooks pretty well.

previously 12
He previously lived in Canada.

probably 12
I'll probably be free on Wednesday.

purpose-built 4/5
It's a new purpose-built museum.

quite + adj 1
She's quite tall.

rapidly 12
When the fire started, he left rapidly.

really + adj 1
He's really kind – I like him a lot.

rectangular 1
It's a rectangular piece of paper.

remarkable 1
She's a remarkable person.

responsible for 3
She's responsible for sales to America.

Index

Your language

restless 1
Laura is very restless, she can't sit still. _____

right opposite 13
The chemist's is right opposite the park. _____

rocky 1
The coastline is very rocky. _____

romantic 1
Romantic stories are all about love. _____

round 1
The letter O is round. _____

run-down 4/5
The buildings are old and run-down. _____

satellite 1
You need a dish to get satellite TV. _____

self-contained 4/5
My flat's self-contained. _____

self-satisfied 4/5
She's so self-satisfied. _____

semi-detached 4/5
They live in a semi-detached house. _____

Index

Your language

seriously ill 1
He's seriously ill. He could die.
_____

shaved head 1
Dave's got a shaved head.
_____

single 1
I'd like a single room, please.
_____

slim 1
He's lost weight. He's slim now.
_____

smashed 4
The windows were all smashed.
_____

smell like 9
This soap smells like roses.
_____

so + adj 1
She's so beautiful – her mother was too.
_____

sort of 14
My young son drew a sort of horse.
_____

sound like 9
That sounds like my car.
_____

spacious 1
It's a spacious house with lots of rooms.
_____

Index

Your language

spicy 1
I love spicy food – the hotter the better. _____

split-level 4/5
I live in a split-level house. _____

square 1
Why is a boxing ring square? _____

state-of-the-art 5
It's a state-of-the-art computer. _____

steady 1
She drove at a steady 50 kph. _____

steep 1
The path up the mountain was steep. _____

straight ahead 12
Just go straight ahead. _____

straight away 12
Bill's ill. Call a doctor straight away. _____

strong-willed 5
I'm strong-willed. I can stop smoking. _____

subsequently 12
He got ill and subsequently died. _____

Index

Your language

successfully 12
They completed the task successfully. _____

superb 1
We had superb wine with the meal. _____

tasteless 1
The soup was tasteless; it needed salt. _____

tasty 1
He made a really tasty meal. _____

tedious 1
The film was so tedious I fell asleep. _____

terribly + adj 1
I'm terribly unhappy. _____

terrifying 4
The film was terrifying. _____

there and back 12
It takes two hours there and back. _____

thrilled to bits 1
Laura was thrilled to bits to get the job. _____

to 10
Here's a box to keep your CDs in. _____

Index

Your language

too + adj (+ to) 7
His car is too big (to go in the garage). _____

to the right 12/13
Turn to the right at the end of the road. _____

two-bedroom 5
They live in a two-bedroom flat. _____

under the weather 13
Phil's a bit under the weather. _____

unlikely 1
Jo is unlikely to come tomorrow. _____

unreliable 1
The trains here are very unreliable. _____

unsatisfactory 1
Their marriage was very unsatisfactory. _____

until 13
I lived in London until 1999. _____

useful 1
A torch is useful when you go camping. _____

very + adj 1
You make me very happy. _____

Index

Your language

walking 4
He nearly died – he's a walking miracle. _____

washing 4
You can use our washing machine. _____

waste-disposal 5
The waste-disposal unit is broken. _____

well acted 4/5
The play was well acted. _____

well-lit 4/5
They live in a well-lit street. _____

well-paid 4/5
She's got a well-paid job. _____

wide-screen 5
We've just bought a wide-screen TV. _____

windy 1
It was so windy I could hardly stand. _____

with 13
I have a flat with two bathrooms. _____

wonderful 1
Pelé was a wonderful footballer. _____

Answers

Review 1
A 1d 2b 3a 4c
B 1 cheaper 2 cheap as 3 cheap
C 1 bad 2 bad 3 bad 4 good

Review 2
A 1d 2c 3a 4b
B 1 average height 2 completely bald 3 overweight
C 1 false 2 true 3 false

Review 3
A 1b 2a 3d 4c
B 1b 2c 3a
C 1b 2a 3a

Review 4
A 1c 2a 3d 4b
B 1 split-level 2 filthy/washing machine 3 open-plan
C 1 to 2 for 3 with

Review 5
A 1d 2c 3b 4a
B 1 unhappy 2 unhappy 3 happy
C 1 true 2 true 3 false

Review 6
A 1 slow 2 fast 3 fast
B 1c 2b 3a
C 1 on foot 2 in the distance 3 convenient for

Review 7
A 1d 2a 3b 4c
B 1 to 2 by 3 in
C 1 true 2 false 3 false

Review 8
A 4, 2, 1, 3
B 1 good 2 good 3 bad
C 1 agree 2 disagree 3 disagree 4 disagree

Review 9
A 1c 2d 3a 4b
B 1 to 2 straight away 3 at the same time as 4 overnight
C 1 false 2 true 3 false

Other titles available in Penguin Quick Guides

Computer English
English Phrasal Verbs
Business English Verbs
Business English Words
Business English Phrases
Making Friends in English
Common Errors in English
Really Useful English Verbs
Really Useful English Words
Really Useful English Idioms
Really Useful English Grammar